FREEDOM AND PLENTY:

OURS TO SAVE

THE MINUTE MEN: THEY DEVELOPED OUR COUNTRY'S PLENTY WHILE EVER READY TO FIGHT FOR OUR NATION'S FREEDOM.

WSB

ON THE LIBERTY BELL WE READ THESE WORDS: *"Proclaim Liberty throughout the land to all the inhabitants thereof "* —

TO WHICH WE MAY ADD: *And let the earth give forth abundance for ourselves and all mankind.*

other books written and illustrated
by Wilfrid S. Bronson

THE WONDER WORLD OF ANTS

CHILDREN OF THE SEA

HORNS AND ANTLERS

STOOPING HAWK AND STRANDED WHALE

THE GRASSHOPPER BOOK

HOOKER'S HOLIDAY

TURTLES

COYOTES

STARLINGS

CATS

FREEDOM AND PLENTY:
OURS TO SAVE

THE CONSERVATION PLEDGE

"*I give my pledge* | *as an American to save and*
faithfully to defend | *from waste the natural resources*
of my country, its | *soil and minerals, its*
forests, waters, and | *wildlife.*"

Written and illustrated by
WILFRID S. BRONSON

HARCOURT, BRACE & WORLD, INC. • NEW YORK

Signing the Declaration

Our Founding Fathers created a "Design for freedom and better living".

COPYRIGHT, 1953, BY WILFRID S. BRONSON

LIBRARY OF CONGRESS CATALOG CARD NUMBER: 52-13252

PRINTED IN THE UNITED STATES OF AMERICA

FREEDOM AND PLENTY:
OURS TO SAVE

I

OUR AMERICA:
WHAT IT MEANS TO US
IN FREEDOM AND IN PLENTY

THERE WAS NOT always a United States of America. Our nation began in 1776. In that year our forefathers wrote the Declaration of Independence. They wrote it to tell the world that Americans did not want to belong to any other nation. They declared that Americans wanted to belong to their own independent nation. For, as they said, everybody has the right to live a free and happy life.

They meant that we Americans should be united as a nation; yet each of us should be free to think, and speak, and do things for ourselves. They meant that every American should be free to think about God in his or her own way.

They meant that any American should be free to say what is not good in our government, without being afraid. We should be free to try to make it better. For we, the people, were to be our own government.

And so we are to this day. Our government is not perfect.

~Reading the Declaration to the people~

No government can be. But it has left us free to make our own mistakes, to learn from them, and to correct them. It has allowed us to work as we pleased, to make the most of happy living. Our many marvelous inventions are the work of free men, working as they pleased. They have given us ever new and better ways of making and doing things. And there are probably more happy people in the United States of America, than anywhere else on earth.

But a free and happy life depends on more than declaring our rights and making fine inventions. It depends on how well we use both our rights and the land we live on. For America is both a nation and a country. As a nation it is something we feel in our hearts, and love. It is our will to preserve freedom and happiness, not only for ourselves, but for the Americans to follow us in years to come. These are things we believe in, the ideals we share as a nation.

But America as a country is something we can see and touch. It is the land beneath our feet, the "rocks and rills" and "templed hills", the fields and forests, the towns and cities. It is everything we grow, or make and use, from radishes to radar, from scallions to skyscrapers. These are things we share as a country.

After our forefathers made their Declaration, they had to fight and win the War for Independence. Since then our great-grandfathers, grandfathers, and our fathers have had

to fight several other wars to preserve our rights and liberty, to save America the nation. But America, the country, needs preserving too. Our land, the very soil America is made of, can be saved, or wasted. It can be worn out and washed into the sea. Or it can be used well and wisely so that we can go on and on, a strong, rich country and a happy nation.

The nation's freedom and the country's plenty must be preserved together. For no one, however free, can live without food. And even with plenty of food, we cannot live well without good clothing, good buildings to dwell and work in, and all the thousands of other good things we use every day of our lives. Freedom is something precious that has grown in our minds as a nation. Food for our bodies must come from plants grown in the soil of our country. Fruits and vegetables, and grain for making flour, all come from plants growing in the soil. Sugar comes from cane, beets, and maple trees. Bees make honey from the nectar of flowers. Eggs, meat, and milk come from farm birds and animals, which are fed on grain and grasses grown in the soil.

Besides food, we get from farm birds and animals such useful stuffs as down and feathers, leather and wool, for com-

fortable bedding and clothes, and so on. Cotton plants likewise provide us with cloth, as well as cordage, cattle-feed, oil, and plastics. And then, also growing in the soil are the forests, which supply us with wood and lumber for buildings, furniture, telegraph poles, pilings, railroad ties, and the like, besides wood-pulp for making the paper and cardboard we use in so many articles. From several kinds of pine trees, we get turpentine and resin, used in paints and varnishes, soap, and medicine. Natural rubber is made from latex, a thick juice taken from rubber trees and various other plants, growing of course in soil.

Turkeys

Cotton

If we use our soil well, so that it remains rich and doesn't wash away with every rain, and if we cut our forests wisely, so that new trees are ready for the mill year after year, we need never run out of food or clothes or things that forests can supply. For everything that grows, whether plant or animal, renews its kind over and over. Each kind multiplies itself by making seeds or laying eggs, or having young ones. A farmer can eat some of this year's wheat and save some for seed for next year's wheat. His old cow gave milk and had a calf each year for ten years. Though she is roast beef now, her calves are cows and are giving milk and having calves themselves. Thus, if managed wisely, our supplies of useful plants and animals that grow and multiply will last and last.

7

If one ear of corn has 300 kernels - and each kernel (planted) makes 2 ears of 300 kernels - that will be 600 ears, or 180,000 kernels.

a lot of corn

Alice

IF ONE COW HAS ONE CALF A YEAR FOR 10 YEARS, AND EACH CALF (GROWN UP) HAS 10 CALVES, THAT WILL BE 100 COWS. A GOOD DAIRY HERD!

Alex

WSB

Of course this applies to our wild creatures also, to our wild birds and mammals, fresh and salt-water fishes, reptiles—in fact to all our wildlife. Many Americans fish for fun, but many others fish to supply the markets, and make their living at it. Much meat and fur is taken by people who trap and hunt all kinds of wild animals, from squirrels up to whales. If the wild things are not over-fished, over-trapped, or over-hunted, and if they are not disturbed when laying eggs or raising young ones, we may always have the kind of food and clothing wild creatures can supply. And for the many Americans who enjoy hunting only with a camera, who love nature for its own sake and prefer watching wildlife undisturbed, there will always be some left for their pleasure and their studies.

8

But we have many needs that cannot be supplied by things that grow and multiply. For these needs we have still other supplies in the earth, some near the surface, some deep down among great layers of rock. These are the minerals, the metals and fuels we dig from mines or pump from wells. Unlike plants and animals, our supplies of coal and oil, metals and

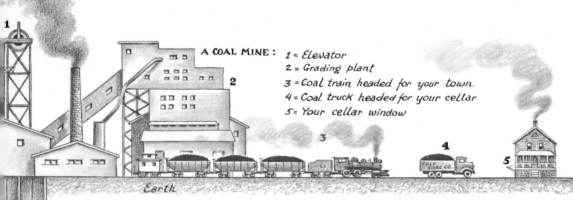

A COAL MINE :
1 = Elevator
2 = Grading plant
3 = Coal train headed for your town
4 = Coal truck headed for your cellar
5 = Your cellar window

Earth

other minerals, cannot renew themselves. These precious stuffs can be used up completely. When we have dug all the coal or iron out of a mine, that mine is empty. After all the oil is pumped from a well, that well is dry. But though our supplies of these things are limited, we need and use great quantities of them every day.

Just think of all the things we make with steel, which is

Layers of coal between layers of rock

made from iron. There are bridges, big buildings, ships, trains, tracks, tractors, cars, pots and pans, tools, weapons, and so on. Think how our homes and the buildings in towns and cities are heated with coal, gas, or oil. Think of all our millions of metal cars and other machines, using coal, gas, oil, and gasoline all over our country all of the time. It is easy to see

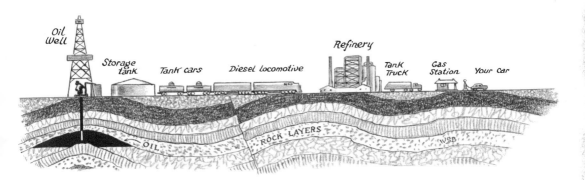

that we should use our limited supplies of all these things as carefully as we can. In fact, we must learn to use all our resources, our metals and other minerals, our forests and wild-life, and the soil of our farms, wisely and not wastefully. We all must learn to do this if we are to save the plenty and the freedom of America, to make it last and last a long, long time.

II
HOW AMERICA GREW:
THE NATION RICHER, THE COUNTRY POORER

LEARNING TO USE things carefully, wisely, and well is not easy for many Americans. This is because it means changing the ways and habits we have had since our first settlers came here from Europe. That was over three hundred years ago. All that time we Americans have been free to make our own mistakes. And, like people everywhere, we have made many. Perhaps we have made only one really bad mistake. But we have made that one so often and in so many ways that by now it is a very big and bad mistake indeed.

For three hundred years and more we have been (and many of us still are) very wasteful people. Though always ready to fight for our nation's freedom, we have been steadily spoiling much of our country's plenty. Though using weapons ably to defend ourselves in war time, we have badly injured ourselves by the unwise use of tools at all times.

TOOLS, UNWISELY USED, MAY DO MORE DAMAGE THAN THE WEAPONS OF AN ENEMY.

Starting westward from our first settlements in Massachusetts and Virginia, with saws and axes, spades and picks, plows, fire, guns and dynamite, we have wasted the good things of America, clear to, yes, even into, the Pacific Ocean.

Now, there are only certain places in our lakes and rivers and the sea where fishes can grow to goodly size and multiply. On the land we have only so much soil that is fit for farms and ranches. Forests can supply just so much wood and lumber yearly. And underground there is just so much iron, oil, and the like, and no more.

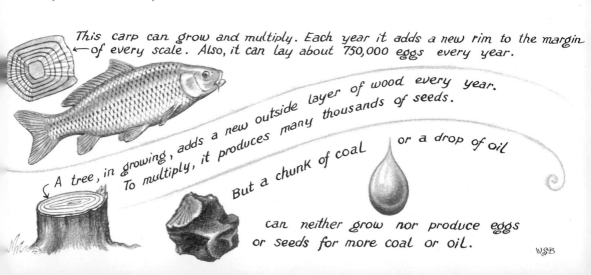

This carp can grow and multiply. Each year it adds a new rim to the margin of every scale. Also, it can lay about 750,000 eggs every year.

A tree, in growing, adds a new outside layer of wood every year. To multiply, it produces many thousands of seeds.

But a chunk of coal or a drop of oil can neither grow nor produce eggs or seeds for more coal or oil.

The more wastefully
we use up what there is,

IRON ORE

the sooner

Only a
ghost

we shall need what there is not. WSB

But every year there are more and more Americans. Millions more people are born than die, and all of them must have more food, more clothing, more houses and schools, and more of everything. We do have more than the people of almost any other nation. But while we grow richer in things for today, we grow poorer in supplies for making more things later on. We know our supplies are limited. Yet we go right on wastefully using them up, faster and faster. So what is to become of us all, and of our America, after a little while?

Well, luckily, we still are free not only to make our own mistakes, but to learn from them. What we must learn is to conserve. To conserve means to save. So to conserve what is left of all our supplies, our natural resources, means to use them savingly and wisely instead of wastefully. This is called conservation, a good old idea in some countries but rather

In mountainous lands, (like Peru or Japan or Switzerland), people have known for ages how to keep precious soil and water from washing away.

new to us here. We Americans pride ourselves on being quick to take up good ideas. We are proud of what we call our "know-how" in making and doing things. But good conservation calls for far more know-how than many of us yet are using.

When we sing "My country 'tis of thee, sweet land of liberty," or "God bless America," we are really counting our blessings. We are thinking of the blessings of freedom and plenty our forefathers found when they came and settled here. Let's just look back for a few minutes to those early times, and see how Americans have used, or abused, their blessings from then till now. We shall see that while building up the nation, we have been tearing down the country by our wasteful ways. Then, later on, we can see what has been done, is being done, and what must yet be done to make things better.

15

When our first settlers arrived from Europe, the country was, of course, completely wild. Much of it was covered with great forests of tall trees. The American Indians, living in the forests, cut very few big trees with their stone hatchets. Here and there they did burn out a little clearing for a corn and pumpkin patch, or a tobacco patch. But—though they invented smoking—they didn't smoke wherever they went, as many of us do. They only smoked about their campfires.

Pole and bark village of forest Indians —

For they had no handy matches, no cigars and cigarettes to toss away still lighted. So they didn't carelessly set the forest blazing in hundreds of places every summer, as some of us do now.

The forest was the Indians' natural home, and so, like the wild animals they hunted there, they had no wish to destroy it. There were seldom many of these very first Americans in any one part of the forest. And every now and then they moved their camps. Their villages did not grow in the same place for centuries the way ours do, needing always larger supplies of wood and lumber. The Indians needed only light poles and bark for their wigwams, canoes, and weapons. They gathered mostly dead wood for their fires. Thus when the first settlers reached America, there stood the mighty trees all up and down the whole Atlantic shore, dense forests that grew inland farther than anyone could even guess.

"If you know where to look," the friendly Indians told the settlers, "you can find anything you need in the forest." This was true for Indians. But for the newcomers there was too much forest, "too much of a good thing." For building and warming their houses, they would need some trees, of course, but they wanted lots of open land for farming, too. They needed room for garden crops, for grain fields, and for pastures. Therefore, much of that solid forest was actually in their way. They had wood to waste, and at first they had to waste it. It looked then as though there would be more than enough for every need, forever.

So, with their saws and axes, and with fire, the settlers cleared the woods away for miles around. This must have surprised the Indians, and undoubtedly it led to trouble. They had made us welcome to share the forests, their home and hunting grounds. But they didn't expect us to start right in destroying them. The Indians had no private property except the few things they made for themselves. The land with its trees, its waters, and its wildlife belonged to all. They believed that the birds and beasts of prey had as much right to live and hunt there as they did themselves. It was no one's right to ruin what belonged to everybody, or to kill more

18

game than could be used. But these pale-faced strangers, besides killing many turkeys, deer, buffalo, etc., never missed a chance to shoot an owl or hawk, a wolf or bear, a bobcat or panther, with their amazing thunder-sticks.

Of course many settlers may have thought it fun to hunt and kill the birds and beasts of prey. But they did it also to make things safer for their own farm animals. The Indians began to see more and more of the strange tame creatures from across the sea; horses, cows, sheep, hogs, to say nothing of dogs and cats. Meanwhile we kept right on helping ourselves to deer and other game. So it is no wonder that a hungry Indian helped himself to a sheep now and then, as needed. Remember, to him meat was meat, to be shared by all. He would not point out a deer and say, "That's mine. Leave it alone." But he soon found that a settler would so claim a sheep.

An Indian taking farm animals looked as bad to a settler as a wolf or a panther doing it. It is sad to think how soon after the first Thanksgiving, when

Indians and settlers ate in peace together, the misunderstandings and fighting began. But from then on there was seldom peace, as Indians and wildlife retreated deeper into the wilderness before the axes, plows, picks, and guns of advancing pioneers.

As our people increased in numbers, and more settlers came from Europe, they needed ever more room. Towns grew up, with mills, workshops, and stores, along the coast at first, but more and more inland as settlers opened the country. They cut always farther westward into the forest. They cut wastefully and then farmed wastefully, with what bad results we shall see in Chapter III. For in all the great wild country there never seemed to be a need to work savingly; they saw no need to conserve the wood supply, or the soil, or anything at all. When a piece of land wore out, they just opened up some more a little farther west, and repeated their mistakes all over again.

Though the pioneers and settlers killed many wild birds and animals for food, they slaughtered millions more just for the "fun" of it. They had no laws for taking fish and game, in those days. And at first there were so many wild birds as sometimes, when in flight, to darken the sky for miles. So it seemed like harmless sport (except to the birds) to see who could knock down the most in a day. The pioneers soon had Indians wasting wildlife too. They offered them guns, steel knives and hatchets, pretty beads and cloth, for all the furs they could get by trapping.

To have these things, instead of using bows and arrows and stone knives, a good many Indians broke their own good conservation rules. They trapped millions more animals than they could ever use for food, hides and fur. Our traders, getting furs so cheaply from the Indians, sold them in Europe for high prices. This profitable business grew and grew until many fur-bearing animals were trapped almost to the last one of their kind.

For a great many years in Europe, gentlemen were not well dressed without a hat of beaver, trapped in America.

And so we went, wastefully ever westward, the nation spreading over the country. As years passed we outgrew the eastern forests, moving onto the grassy prairies of the middle-west. Here was a wondrous land for farming, just waiting for our plows. Many of us settled here, but always there were others moving on. We crossed the western plains, setting up tremendous cattle ranches. As wasteful as ever, we first killed off millions of buffalo and antelope, then tried to raise more cows than the range land could feed. From much over-grazing, a lot of good land was turned into useless desert.

It kept getting easier and easier for more and more people to go west. For, not far behind the clumsy covered wagons and the stagecoaches, came the railroads, carrying all manner of goods and the different sorts of people who always follow

pioneers and prospectors, and set up new communities. Among these were the workingmen of various trades—merchants, ministers, gamblers, cow-men, miners, women and children. There were cow towns, lumbermill towns, and mining towns. By 1849, mining towns had sprung up in the western mountains clear to California, where gold and other precious metals had been found.

At last America reached "from sea to shining sea," great in size and in the number of its restless people. In only about two centuries we had grown from two little colonies of a few hundred people into a mighty nation. From three-and-a-half million square miles of wilderness, we had hacked out a country that spread from the Atlantic to the Pacific, from the Great Lakes to the Gulf of Mexico. If we had hacked

It must have been hard for young Abe Lincoln to study by a pine knot's light.

less, worked more savingly, and grown less rapidly, things might have been far better. But in 1850, it must still have seemed to almost everyone that we were living in a land which never could run out of riches. It seems so to many of us even now, a hundred years and more since we swarmed into Washington, and Oregon, and California. It surely looks that way to people in less happy lands across the seas.

But it really is not so. We can run out of riches. As we were wasteful in other days, we still are. Only today, the very inventions that make living easier than in pioneering times make it much easier also to use up and wear out what supplies and resources we have left. From the first settlers' candles or sputtering pine-knots, we have advanced to whale-oil lamps, to kerosene lamps, to gaslight, to electric light.

24

But now, though we have electric lights, it is hard for us to study because of television.

With electricity we now can run a million gadgets that we never could before. Electricity sparks more and more machines that eat up ever more fuel and use up more materials ever faster. From horse-drawn vehicles and sailing vessels we have changed to steam-driven railroad trains and ships, burning coal and oil, and to gasoline-driven cars, trucks, busses, and jet-driven planes.

We have all manner of machines to make still other machines that can use up our supplies more rapidly. We can dig and pump more minerals out of the ground in a day than ever before. We can cut more trees and mill them faster and ship the lumber farther sooner. We can plow more land and take bigger crops from the soil with fewer men to do the work. In a few hours we can fly to the remotest area

of remaining wilderness. There, with marvelous modern rifles and telescopic sights, we can shoot the shiest creatures from afar. No forest, no matter how far from settled country, is any longer safe from a careless camper's matches. If wild birds and animals could sing any of our human songs, they surely would select "There Ain't No Hidin' Place." For such is certainly the case.

So it is clear that we are now more able than ever to ruin our own beautiful, bountiful part of the world. Therefore we need, as never before, to make sure no such terrible thing takes place. Some things have been done and are being done to conserve our supplies, and so to save America. Before we see what these good measures are, and what more must be done, let us look at a river basin, a whole river valley where many bad mistakes of wastefulness have been and still are being made. The sight will be a most unpleasant one, but we must face our troubles squarely, if we would find the remedies.

When the wind is right, you can tell you're nearing home long before you can see any land.

III

VALLEY OF THE RIVER MUDDYFLOW

LET'S BEGIN where the river does, high in the mountains at the valley's upper end. We can follow the river all the way down to the sea, observing the wasteful errors of the valley people. It would be impossible to decide who has done most to make a mess of things, so many have done so much. Everybody's bad judgment has made misery for almost everybody else.

Once the mountain at the head of the valley was covered

with a splendid forest. Then a lumberman bought up all that cheap, wild, lofty land, and quickly went to cutting the trees. He could have taken timber carefully and wisely. He could have cut only trees that were really ready for the mill, leaving the rest to grow larger and to make seeds for new trees. Thus he could have kept a healthy forest growing steadily, while making money for him year after year.

But, as so often happens, the owner couldn't think very far ahead, or perhaps he didn't want to. Maybe all he wanted was to get as much money from the forest as he could right away, the year he bought it. Never mind about the years and years to follow. Whatever the reason, he cut and sold every tree, big and little, on the mountain as fast as possible. He may have made quite a lot of money, just that once. But it could never be as much as if the lumber had been properly cut, year after year. Also, by taking all the trees at once, he ruined the home of wild birds and animals. We now have laws to protect many of them from too much hunting and trapping. But such laws are of little use where we can't save the homes of woodland creatures from being destroyed in this way. Those animals that could, most certainly went elsewhere. And as for people who love the out-of-doors, there could be no more hiking, camping, or picnicking in the once pleasant forest.

Very seldom can we waste one thing without wasting other things, things that perhaps belong to somebody else. The wasteful lumberman not only spoiled his forest, the homes of wildlife, and the pleasure of other people; the rubbish left all over the mountain was like a mighty heap of kindling wood. About a year after the forest was all cut down, the autumn came on very dry. During a nearly rainless thunderstorm, the lightning struck that matchstick-covered mountain and set it blazing. The fire spread to the permanent forest on a nearby mountain owned by a better lumberman, who cut more wisely. It burned much of this standing forest, including a little vacation resort town located there.

The mountain forest had been a water regulator. The leaves and twigs, branches and boughs, and the bark of its tree trunks, caught and slowed and held much of the falling rain. The soft, spongy forest floor, all made of moldering leaves, rotted bark, etc., soaked up even more of the rain. It kept the water from running down the mountain slopes all at once in a flood. It kept the rain from cutting into the soil and washing it away down the mountain. The forest let even the hardest rain down more slowly, more gently. It let some of the water sink slowly but steadily and deeply through the earth. Then a few miles down the mountain, the same water bubbled out of the ground as a clear cold spring, fine for drinking.

A little forest brook flowed from this spring, carrying no soil away, but running clear the year around. Farther down the mountain, where it became a goodly stream, it still ran clear. But with the forest cut and burned away, the mountain now lies all uncovered. The once

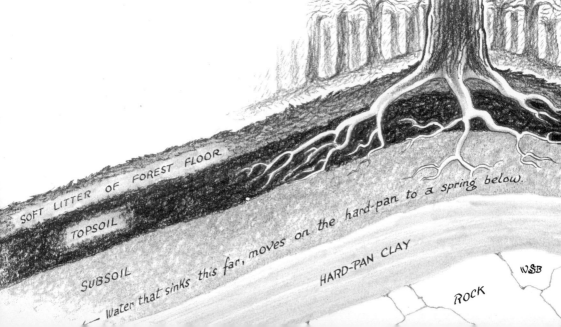

Raindrops are spread on every leaf, stem, twig, branch, bough, and on the trunk. They are caught in every crotch & in every crevice of the bark. Drops are soaked up by the roots and by the forest litter, the topsoil, and subsoil.

SOFT LITTER OF FOREST FLOOR

TOPSOIL

SUBSOIL

Water that sinks this far, moves on the hard-pan to a spring below.

HARD-PAN CLAY

ROCK

WSB

clear brook and stream now run too fast and muddily when it rains, and then dry up. Thousands of fishes are left high and dry when the flooding stream dries quickly. They all lose their lives, and nobody gets a chance to catch a few for dinner.

(Except, possibly, crows)

DRYING STREAM

DRYING MUD-HOLE

DRYING STREAM-BED

The mountain is eroding badly. With every rain it loses soil, washed away with the water. The rich topsoil that was once the forest floor is gone already. Now the gravelly clay subsoil is going. Great gullies grow and grow as every raindrop helps to dig them deeper, wider and longer. Lesser gullies fork out and out from the bigger ones. Nature, carving in the mud, seems to be making hollow, branching models of the departed trees. The mountain, being stripped to the rocks beneath its moving soil, is ever less able to grow any big new trees.

People living below the barren mountain have to drill deep wells to get any drinking water now. Or, like the wild animals, they have to move away. Indeed, unless they move away, their homes may be undermined by the giant creeping gullies, and topple in. Now, during the heavy rain, far down the valley where the stream becomes a river, farms are flooded with muddy water running off, too fast, from the naked mountain. And when the flood is gone, pastures and hay fields and crops lie ruined, weighed down with the sticky clay.

But besides this, the valley farmers have their own ways of wasting soil and water.

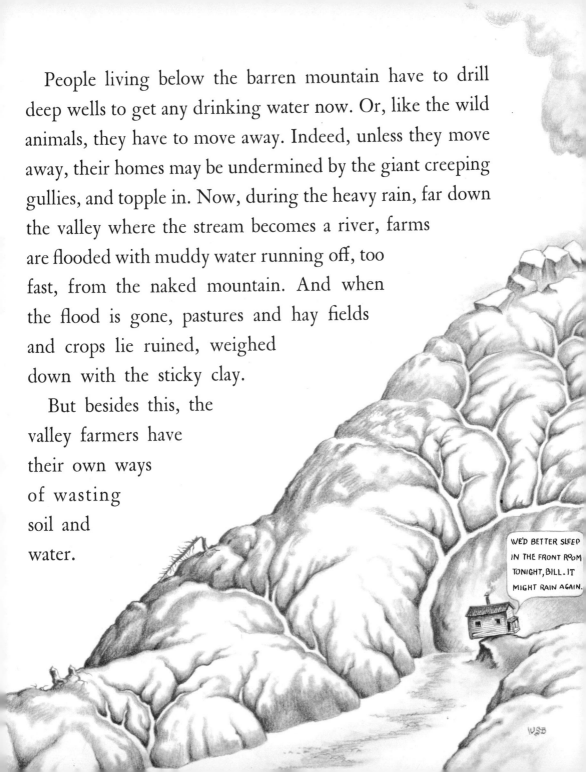

WE'D BETTER SLEEP IN THE FRONT ROOM TONIGHT, BILL. IT MIGHT RAIN AGAIN.

That's Farmer X. He's wearing out his horse, himself, and his land.

WHAT SOIL DOESN'T WASH AWAY THROUGH THE CULVERT IS CLEANED FROM ROADSIDE DITCHES AND TRUCKED AWAY BY HIGHWAY CREWS. IT IS NOT PUT BACK ON FARMER X'S FIELDS.

"You can't fit a square peg into a round hole," any of them would say. Yet all make trouble for themselves by trying to fit square fields to rounding hills. Instead of plowing around the hills, following their true form, and keeping the furrows level, the farmers plow their square fields up and down the slopes. And so the rain, far from being held where it falls to soak into the ground, runs right down the slanting furrows and out of the fields. With the water much precious soil is washed away, carried down to the river, the River Muddy-flow, and finally to the sea.

Some of the farmers lose soil also by grazing too many cattle, and especially too many sheep. Good lush grass holds soil together and keeps it moist, by sponging up the rain, just as forests do. But if there are too many hungry animals

34

No silt in these ditches since he's been plowing by the contours. He gets into town now — with money to spend!

NOT MUCH WATER FLOWS, AND NO SOIL PASSES THROUGH THE CULVERT NOW. THE GULLY IS FILLED. THE PASTURE IS ON THE STEEPER SLOPES.

for the size of the fields, they keep every blade of grass clipped off close to the ground. Sheep and goats even nibble the roots.

Even if the farmers plowed properly around, not up and down the hills, and never over-grazed their pastures, many would still wear out their land. For year after year they plant the same crops in the same fields, instead of shifting, say, from corn to wheat to clover and back to corn. Every summer, fields planted always to corn, for example, give shorter stalks with fewer ears until there is nothing left in that ground for corn to feed and grow on.

It is getting harder and harder for anyone to make a living in such a wasted countryside. The towns, like the surrounding farms, are growing ever poorer too. Lumber mills and paper mills are closing down for lack of timber and pulpwood. The owners, the lumberjacks, and the mill-hands, are all out of jobs. The milk companies are failing with the same result. Trade is coming to a stand-still, for people have no money to spend. Stores close. So do the schools. Buildings don't get repaired, and so the towns look sadder and sadder. They shrink and shrink, as townspeople and farmers move away.

But new land to waste is harder and harder to find. We can no longer just pack up and go farther west. People are already there, wasting the land and its products, as in all parts of our country. So more and more of the valley people look for work in the bigger cities down the Muddyflow. There they make the same mistakes of wastefulness in many new ways, though for the same old reasons. Some don't know any better, some

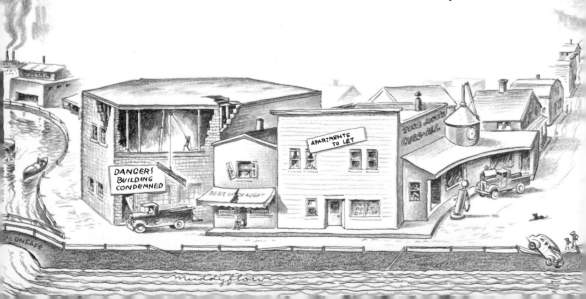

don't think what they do can matter much, and some simply do not care.

Cities need a sure supply of good clean water, millions of gallons every day. People must drink, cook, bathe, wash clothes, sprinkle lawns, etc. Much water is needed for public swimming pools, for air-conditioning in buildings, for fighting fires, washing streets, and flushing sewers. Many factories in the cities use lots of water too. The Muddyflow can furnish more water than all the river cities need, but its water is not fit to use. For, adding to the mud from wasted farms and forests, the cities dump their garbage and empty their sewers into the river. Their factories pour in poisonous liquids, left from the work of making things. This fouling and poisoning is called stream pollution. The water, passing each city farther

down the stream, gets ever dirtier and more polluted.

Where the Muddyflow enters the sea, a very big city pours its sewage and factory poisons into the harbor. It would dump its rubbish and garbage there also, if the tide would carry it away. But, unlike the river, the ocean tide flows out and back again. So this sea-coast city loads its refuse onto barges; then tugboats tow it out to dump in deep sea water. But they don't go far enough, and much of it floats back. It washes up on beaches all along the coast. Bathing is impossible anyway because of the filth steadily entering the sea from the river.

A breeze, blowing over tidal marshes, no longer smells of sweet grasses. With very good sense, the marsh birds no longer try to live there. Migrating water-fowl fly on to cleaner places. Only a few dingy gulls remain, living on refuse. The

river fishes all have died. And sea fishes, like shad and salmon, no longer try to swim upstream each year to lay their eggs.

Sometimes during heavy rains, when swollen brooks rush to the River Muddyflow, it rises above its banks and swamps the cities. The high water swirls through the streets, carrying every loose thing with it. Food, and other goods in stores, is spoiled. In houses, wallpaper comes loose. The paste is soaked. So is the glue in furniture. Chairs and tables fall apart. Musical instruments, radios, and television sets will never play again. Rugs and mattresses ooze muddy water. It will be months before these ruined things can all be cleared away. Every furnace, and every engine of cars and trucks caught in the flood, must be taken apart and cleaned.

It almost seems as though nature tries every now and then to flush the whole Muddyflow valley and the river clean. But this only spreads filth far and wide. Drowned animals lie about everywhere. All drinking water is poisoned. There is no gas or electricity, or even dry wood, for boiling it. Good Americans, from outside the flooded valley, bring in clean water, food, blankets, medicine, and help all they can. The Red Cross, the National Guard, the Coast Guard, supported by all of us, help when a flood is bad enough. Floods cost every American dearly whether we live in the troubled area or elsewhere.

Years ago the Government—that means every American —built a big expensive dam across the Muddyflow to hold

back the flooding water. But the dam soon filled with mud, soil lost from the wasted lands above it. So now it neither holds back the floods nor stores any extra water for times of drought. And the money it cost to build, the time and work, and the steel and concrete all were wasted. For a decent water supply some cities have had to drill deep wells and set up big expensive pumping stations. Others have built reservoirs a hundred miles or so away, among brooks in mountains not yet spoiled by wasteful lumbering.

The cities by the River Muddyflow make other bad mistakes of wastefulness. They poison not only the water in the river but the very air their people breathe. Day and night from thousands of chimneys, private dwellings, public buildings, factories and refineries, come clouds of smoke. And with the smoke—besides grit, soot, and poisonous fumes—come tons and tons of costly chemicals. The chemicals, needed for making many useful things, are being wasted. They could be separated from the smoke and saved.

Not only is the smoke bad to breathe, it makes buildings dull and dingy inside and out, and soils everybody's clothing. It shuts out so much sunshine that plants die in window boxes, and people working outdoors never tan. Aviators, try-

MUCH HEAT GOING UP CHIMNEYS CAN BE RE-USED ALSO — SAVING ON AMOUNT OF FUELS NEEDED.

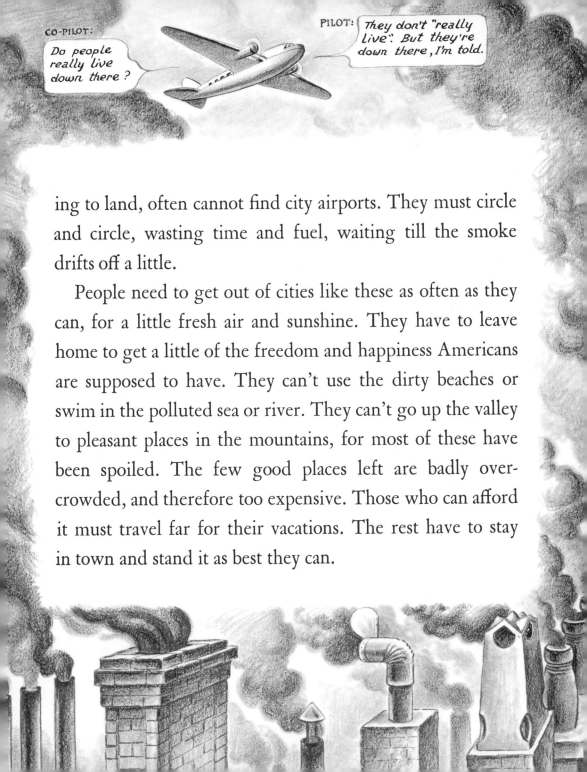

CO-PILOT: Do people really live down there?

PILOT: They don't "really live". But they're down there, I'm told.

ing to land, often cannot find city airports. They must circle and circle, wasting time and fuel, waiting till the smoke drifts off a little.

People need to get out of cities like these as often as they can, for a little fresh air and sunshine. They have to leave home to get a little of the freedom and happiness Americans are supposed to have. They can't use the dirty beaches or swim in the polluted sea or river. They can't go up the valley to pleasant places in the mountains, for most of these have been spoiled. The few good places left are badly over-crowded, and therefore too expensive. Those who can afford it must travel far for their vacations. The rest have to stay in town and stand it as best they can.

IV

THE CLEARGOOD RIVER VALLEY

HOW IN THE WORLD did the people of Muddyflow Valley, U.S.A. ever get into such a sorry state? Well, as we said before, we Americans are proud of our "know-how." But actually only some of our citizens have it. To be better Americans, millions more of us need to "know-how" to work less wastefully, more wisely. We need to "know-how" conservation can save our plenty, protect our freedom, and preserve our happiness. And there is no good excuse for our not finding out. Our National Government—for the whole nation—our State Governments, many of our county, city and village governments, foresters', farmers', sportsmen's clubs, boys' clubs, girls' clubs, our schools and colleges, and outdoor magazines, are all teaching Conservation. They are

trying to get all Americans to use the land and its products savingly. For only when each one of us learns to live this way, will the liberty and happiness of all be safe. Any good American should gladly make to himself and his fellow countrymen the Conservation Pledge, given on our title page, and should always try to live up to it.

Like anyone else, the unhappy people of Muddyflow Valley can learn that what each American does makes a difference to all his countrymen. They can see that though a forest or a farm may be just one man's property, it is also a part of the whole United States. They can see that if the

45

owner wastes his soil, he is also wasting the beloved country that belongs to all of us. They can be made to see that one city, polluting a river which flows to other cities, is as wicked as one man poisoning another man's well. So let's see what is to be done. What can the people do to earn the name of "Cleargood" for their river valley, instead of Muddyflow?

Relief map of River Project

Well, for one thing, since the old dam is useless, they will need a new one. But this time they won't just go ahead and build a dam. Leading valley citizens will work with Government experts to make a big all-over plan. They will study everybody's needs, and everything being done in the valley from the mountains to the sea. For the new dam must not fill with mud like the old one. Before it is built, forests will have to be managed more wisely. There will, of course, be forest rangers always on the look-out. But people will learn to be more careful with fire in the woods. They will not complain if the woods are closed during long and dangerous dry spells. Where the mountains are bare, new forests must be planted. This will slow the run-off of the rain and cause cool steady springs and brooks to flow again. Once more birds and wild animals will find good places there for homes and hide-outs.

The tame, grazing animals of farms will be fenced out of the forests. Then seedlings, instead of being eaten, can grow into fine tall trees. Farmers finally will learn that it doesn't pay to over-graze their pastures. They will stop up the awful gullies where their land keeps wasting away. And they will plow by the contours so as to lose no more soil, but improve what is left. Thus the new dam will fill more slowly but with only the clearest water. Some of this water, stored above the dam, will be used to irrigate, to wet land below the dam too dry for farming now. And no longer will costly fuels be burned to turn the wheels that make electric power. Water, passing through the dam, will turn them. Electricity will be cheaper on the farms as well as in the cities now, all through the valley.

There will be locks around the dam to let boats pass, boats carrying merchandise, and boats carrying happy people on vacations, who will tour, swim, boat, skate, ski, hike, camp, hunt in season, study nature, or just rest in the mountains. For not only the water in the new dam, but the whole countryside will be clean again. People will be free once more to find a little happiness.

FREE PARKING

TRADER

CLEARGOOD LOCKS

TO BATHING PAVILION

BUSINESS
AND PLEASURE ON THE
CLEARGOOD RIVER

The garbage of towns and cities will be turned into fertilizer, along with the scraps from all food canneries. And each town will have a sewage treating plant. These will change the poisonous sewage into harmless topsoil, the very best, to be put back on wasted farmlands. All factories will treat the liquids they throw out, to make them also harmless. Smoke will be treated and controlled. The sea coast will be clean and sweet again. People can bathe in the water or tan in the sun, and the birds will all come back. Year in and year out the river, now called the Cleargood, will furnish water for every use in town and country, all up and down the valley. And such a valley will be a part of our America, saved.

But wait a minute! We still haven't thought of every possible thing to improve the valley. We have planned how to lessen the damage floods may do. But we haven't ended all floods. In spite of our new dam, and better forestry and farming, it can and will rain so hard and so long sometimes that we shall have floods now and again. And we had better face that fact. Floods won't carry away as much precious soil as they used to. And they won't come so often. But when they do come, people can still be drowned, or lose their homes, and property can still be damaged.

In years gone by, the cities in this valley had to be where they are, right by the river. Almost everything came to them by boat, for roads were very few and very poor. Besides, they needed water-power for their mills. But now, with trucks, busses, railroads and planes, river traffic is not so necessary. And electric power—though made by water power—can be used far from the river. *So why not move the cities out of the way of any more possible floods?*

It will take years to do, of course. But it will cost less than the damage sure to be done by floods in the future. All new buildings will be set back from the river on high ground. Gradually block after block of the old buildings will be torn down. Where they stood, the lowlands can be farmed or made into spacious city parks. Areas can be set apart for wild birds and beasts. There, protected from hunters, they will live their interesting lives less and less afraid of tourists and nature-students watching them.

Broken stones and concrete rubble from the torn-down buildings can be sunk in the sea beyond the harbor of the coastal city. This will form a fine fish rockery, where people can go in boats for the fun of catching their own sea food on holidays. When all this has at last been done, the Cleargood River Valley, or any valley like it, will be indeed a lovely part of our America, saved.

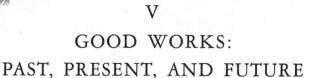

V
GOOD WORKS:
PAST, PRESENT, AND FUTURE

A LOT OF PEOPLE cannot recognize a crisis unless someone is in bodily danger. A lady screaming on a runaway horse is exciting, and everyone agrees the horse must be stopped. But runaway land, moving more slowly and quietly, is really a greater danger to more people. Accidentally the frightened horse may end the life of the helpless lady, but runaway land can take away the living of millions of people. Yet many citizens, who would move quickly to control a horse running away with a lady, may do nothing to control water running away with our soil.

It is easier to lead people in preserving their nation than in conserving their country. When Paul Revere rode shouting through the night, men left their beds and hurried out to fight the first battle of our War for Independence. Then for seven years they fought on, following General Washington. They trusted his judgment and did his bidding until the war was won. But in more peaceful years, when leaders like Washington urged Americans to save their soil by plowing around the hills, they paid no heed but went wastefully on plowing them up and down. So it has been and still is with many Americans. A man may become a willing soldier when called by his War Department, yet be stubborn and unheeding when advised by his Conservation Department.

That is one reason there still are many regions in our United States too much like the Muddyflow Valley. None of them need to be. Sensible, patriotic people anywhere can improve the districts where they live and work. Experts from the National or the State Conservation Departments will help them make a good all-over plan, free of charge. Then everyone in the district can vote for or against the plan.

If a few are against it, if they refuse to end their wasteful ways, harming themselves and others, they can be persuaded. If some land-owner won't block up his gullies and plant shrubs and vines there to stop soil from washing down, muddying streams and farms below, the district can fix the gullies and charge him for the work. When warned of this, he may get busy and fix them himself. Later on, though perhaps never admitting it, he is likely to be glad he did.

There is always some one who will act selfishly unless persuaded to act otherwise. That is why we have laws, and officers to enforce them. Some time after our plundering people had opened the country from sea to sea, some of our wise leaders recognized a crisis. They saw that, like runaway horses, our own heedless wastefulness could bring us to disaster, unless controlled. They didn't scream like the lady on the horse, but worked hard for laws that would at least bring some control.

Scattered all across the country, by-passed by westward hurrying pioneers, were many large areas as yet untouched by axe, plows, guns or fire. Still unclaimed by any man, they were like islands of unspoiled nature in a sea of mines and lumber camps and ranches. There might be precious minerals underground, but here above ground, for all to see, stood what was left of our once mighty virgin forests. And within these splendid forests, mountains, lakes, and cascading rivers, wild creatures large and small still lived their normal lives unchanged.

Through the good work of those wise leaders, many such magnificent regions were declared National Forests. They

I have protected the deer from "varmints"

Some deer do not look up often enough —

belong to us all. And the only lumbering done in them is managed by our own Government Foresters. These experts show which trees may be taken year by year, so that the forests themselves remain there, growing and making more lumber while still providing haunts for wildlife. Rangers and scientists protect the forests from fire and tree-killing insects and diseases.

Of course all hunting and fishing is controlled by law as well; just so many of a kind to each hunter and fisherman during limited seasons—and none when creatures are raising young ones. Besides this there are sanctuaries and wilderness areas within the National Forests, where no hunting is allowed at any time. Here hunted animals can retire to safety. But also from here, many animals move out into the rest of

56

now I have to rotect them from themselves.

the forest, affording the hunters their chances. It costs money to go hunting, and much of the hunters' tax money is used for the upkeep of these forests.

Some hunting is necessary nowadays. Before settlers killed so many hunting birds and mammals, these meat-eaters caught all weak or sick or careless deer, rabbits, and other vegetable-eating animals. The strong and the keen were left to browse on forest leaves and grasses. With only the best surviving, there was generally ample food for all. But now with meat-eating birds and mammals too scarce to check them, vegetable-eating animals often become too numerous. Human hunters, replacing hawks, owls, wolves, panthers, and the others, have to keep the numbers down. Without one control or the other, rabbits, those rapid multipliers, would soon be eating most of the grass needed for our sheep and cattle. And even deer, though raising but one or two fawns a year, if not hunted, quickly outstrip their food

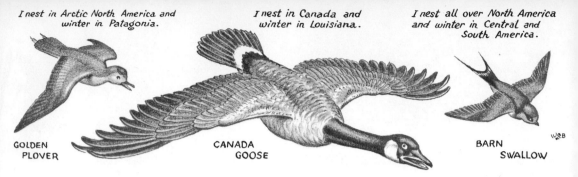

supply. Soon they are cropping every leaf they can reach standing on their hind legs, and every seedling tree or shrub that starts to grow in the forest. Thus no new trees could grow to replace old ones as they die, and the deer would run completely out of food. Then all would starve, the strong with the weak. Where there are too few deer, no hunting is allowed. But where there are too many, some have to be culled out to save the rest.

Hunting and fishing laws are in force everywhere in America. The rules for each area may be changed from year to year, according to how plentiful or scarce the various kinds of fish and game may be. We have set aside safe resting and feeding areas along the fly-ways of birds that go south in winter and north in summer. We have agreements with Canada and Mexico by which we try to protect the birds at each end of their journey. We have agreements with other countries about fishes that also migrate, and about seals, sea otters, and whales. We have laws for the taking of lobsters, oysters, and other shellfish. Thus protected, each kind of creature may survive, and kinds once badly over-hunted or over-fished may increase again. There are always stupid and greedy persons who would gladly kill the last living thing of any kind. The laws not only protect wildlife against such people, but they protect the rights of fair-minded sportsmen and market hunters and fishermen as well. And to some extent they protect the rights of other good Americans who prefer to hunt with cameras, or only with their eyes.

The right to watch and enjoy and study wild creatures in our great outdoors is as important for many of us as the right to hunt them with weapons is to others. For the millions who feel that way and can benefit by it, and for like-minded Americans  who will follow us, we have the National Parks.

A National Park is managed differently from a National Forest. In a National Forest, lumbering and hunting are allowed except in special wildlife refuge areas. But a National Park is all wildlife refuge area, where lumbering and hunting are never allowed. The National Parks are being preserved in their natural state. There are few roads, and places of special interest are reached only by trails.

For those who enjoy outdoor life in other ways besides hunting and fishing, the National Forests again supply the

opportunities, with boating, swimming, camping, hiking, skating, and skiing.

Added to the National Forests and the forests in National Parks, we have state, county, town, and school forests. Following the advice of forestry experts, most of them are managed so that they will yield lumber year after year. Co-operating with the National or State Conservation Departments, they are protected from forest diseases and from fire. If a town or a school wants to start a new forest, or add to one already growing, their Conservation Department will supply thousands of seedling trees, of kinds best suited to each special area. Owners of forests and woodlots on private property can get the same help if they agree to cut their trees like good conservationists. More and more are doing so. And this is good, for

Adding more seedlings to their school forest.

DANGER
CHILDREN
WORKING

every forest used more wisely is another part of our America saved. But there still are many hold-outs, people who prefer to cut like the owner of the forest above the Muddyflow Valley. Private forests still are destroyed, ruining the homes of the wildlife that belongs to everyone, and causing floods that waste our country.

Just as we have public laws for private hunters, to protect our wildlife, maybe we need public laws for private lumbermen, to protect our forests. Every good lumberman would obey these laws, just as all good drivers obey public traffic rules while using their own private cars. This surely would prevent much waste of wood, just as traffic rules prevent many wasteful accidents. It is against the law to scalp a man. There should be a law against scalping a mountain, or other forest land.

Maybe, along with laws for the wise use of forests and forest products, we need some for the saving use of forest by-products—the stuff that is left after the products are made. Some lumbermen are already finding very good uses for the by-products of their business. Timbers too short for lumber are made into baseball bats and tool handles, or split into withes for making baskets. Bark, slabs, and small branches are shredded for bedding in cow barns, or ground up and made into wallboard. Houses built with such material are cooler in the summer, and take less fuel to heat in winter. Sawdust—a by-product from turning trees into lumber— always used to be wasted. But it makes a very good fuel when pressed into compact little bricks. Scientists are working to

make sawdust into good food for cows. Who knows? Maybe they will dish up something people can enjoy eating too.

And further in regard to cows, scientists are making better sprays to keep our livestock free from biting flies, lice and ticks. Comfortable cattle grow bigger, providing more meat and giving more milk on the same amount of hay. With electricity in their barns, some farmers play a radio at milking time. They find that the cows, freed from flies, and happy with soft music, add even more milk to our food supply. It pays to insure a free and happy life, even for American animals.

Clearing poor trees from woodlot.
Cutting ready trees and milling out
lumber, all with portable power-saws.

Plowing ditch to divert water. Ditch to be sodded

Drilling in lime + seed
+ fertilizer, after

Power
post-hole
digger

soil-packer,
after

Setting out a
multiflora rose hedge

Disk plowing

Bulldozer
rounding and
partly filling gully

To teach better ways to farmers who still use Muddyflow methods, our National and State Governments put on wonderful shows. Farmers from all the nearby countryside can come and watch while experts, using plows, bulldozers, graders, brains and muscles, fix up a run-down farm in just one day. They fix it so that it will lose no more soil and have better and better crops from that day on. Any watching farmer, who would like to do the same with his property, can get help from his State Conservation Department.

But as with lumbermen, there still are many hold-out farmers. They go on wasting their topsoil by plowing up and down hill. They still plant the same crops in the same fields every year. And they leave the harvested fields and

Planting seedling trees by machine (1000 per hour).

WELL LOOKA THERE!

This field for hay —

Grader making terraces

This one for row-crops, after clover —

This field for pasture.

CONSERVATION
FIELD-DAY
ALL MACHINERY LOANED BY LOCAL
FARM & ROAD EQUIPMENT DEALERS. ADV.

Plugging gully with rocks

over-grazed pastures bare all winter where a saving blanket of alfalfa, rye, or clover should be growing. If we need a law against scalping forests, we surely need another against skinning farms.

Meanwhile, our scientists have been working on an earth-improving powder. It makes even hard clay subsoils light and spongy. By thus letting in air and water and fertilizer, it makes poor subsoils as good for raising crops as the lost and wasted topsoil was. With gullies fixed, wiser working habits learned, and this powder on his fields, a man should be able to return to his deserted farm, raise much-needed food, and make it pay.

So much for our renewable supplies, produced from things

67

that grow. The more we learn about the care of growing things, the more plentiful those supplies will be. Now, just at random, let's look at a few of our non-renewable supplies. We can only learn to use these as savingly as possible, to make them last. But, as with forest products, we can save a lot by finding uses for the by-products left after making things from these supplies.

While some scientists are seeking better ways to raise oil from wells, others are improving ways to get it out of shale rocks and coal. To cook out the oil and refine it, they burn the gas and tar—by-products—from those same rocks. Another valuable by-product is ashes. Coal ashes are fine fertilizer, wonderful in potato fields. Shale ashes can be used in cement, building blocks, and bricks.

Good old slag! On the fields it gives bigger and better crops. In cinder-blocks it gives a bigger, better hen-house more cheaply and quickly!

Slag, a by-product left from making steel, is no longer heaped in useless mountainous piles. It is mixed with concrete to make cinder blocks for putting up strong buildings quickly and cheaply. And, ground to powder, slag can be used as fertilizer, to enrich the soil. Builders and farmers are glad to get these by-products. And steel companies make money on the slag they used to waste.

69

Like shale, I also am a rock. So, while rocks are speaking, let me just say that, like shale, coal can supply oil and oil products; and I may add ~ heat in your home, the gas in your stove, coke for the steel of many articles, the anti-freeze in your car, the fly-dope in your sprayer, the cloth in your pajamas, the rubber in your mattress, though not yet the dreams in your sleep.

MR. COAL

Steel makers have to use coke. Coke is made by baking the chemicals out of coal. The chemicals, the by-products, are not wasted now. They are made into medicines, plastics, synthetic—not natural—rubber, and thousands of other things. And so it goes. The by-products are often as important as the products. And they are made of stuffs that otherwise would be thrown away.

Some of our inventors are improving ways to turn salt water into fresh. Dry deserts—within piping distance of a sea coast—may thus be made wet again, to grow much-needed food. We are learning to use atomic power to drive machinery and heat houses, among other things. Possibly we can use the waste piles of atomic factories to furnish central

← A drilled steam-well in Italy, — and a distant, smoking volcano ↙

ALREADY IN ITALY, VOLCANIC STEAM FROM DRILLED WELLS TURNS WHEELS TO MAKE ELECTRIC POWER. BUT VOLCANIC HEAT CAN BE USED WITHOUT DRILLING. IN COLDER ICELAND. THERE, VOLCANOES SMOLDERING UNDER ICE-COVERED MOUNTAINS MAKE MUCH HOT WATER UNDERGROUND. THIS HEATS THE SOIL ABOVE, KEEPING SEED-BEDS AND GARDENS WARM, PRODUCING MUCH FOOD. A DISH OF DOUGH, SUNK IN THE SAND, BAKES INTO BREAD. THE HOT WATER, BUB-BLING UP IN SPRINGS, IS PIPED INTO OFFICES, HOMES, LAUNDRIES, AND SO ON. NO FUEL, NO FURNACES TO TEND, NO BILLS TO PAY!

heating for whole cities. Or maybe we can bore down deeply enough to get heat and power from away inside the earth. Hot springs and volcanoes show that there is plenty there. And there is sunlight, from which we are learning to take heat for our homes and power for our machinery. We are learning to make sunlight grow certain plants much more richly and rapidly. Sooner or later we may increase our crops the same way. But whatever wonderful inventions we may make, we shall have to use some of the same non-renewable stuffs—that are steadily growing scarcer—to carry out our new ideas. So we still must be as saving of them as we can.

71

I may be just common clay, the poorest soil for farming, but I'm fine for bricks,— and besides I'll give you Titanium to improve your steel and to make harder, lighter, greater heat-standing parts for jet engines.

We could save a great deal by using less ornamental metal on our automobiles, while giving them even better engines. In place of scarce metals, we can use plastics for many articles. Some metals can be taken from the most surprising places. For example, titanium, a very useful metal, is often found in common clay. Dissolved in sea water is another metal called magnesium. It does not rust, is very strong, but lighter than aluminum. Already ways have been invented to take it from the sea. We can take dissolved gold from the ocean too.

CODFISH

Fishes have been caught with a gold watch or a golden wedding ring (which had fallen overboard), on their insides. But the water on their outsides is full of dissolved gold, (useful for making more rings and watches), as well as magnesium for making ladders, airplanes, and many other things.

IF YOU WONDER WHY I EAT THE JEWELRY OF SEA-SICK TRAVELERS, SEE THE WORD "OM-NI-VO-ROUS" IN YOUR DICTIONARY.

In new steel, a ruined tank may serve again, for some peaceful purpose.

Of course we can save metals and some other materials by using them over again. Though we have had to fight wasteful wars in defense of freedom, we can at least recover some of the metals spent in fighting. Broken armor can be collected from the battlefields, and sunken ships with their precious cargoes can be raised from shallow seas. An old wood-burning, cast-iron stove is not useless, though we are cooking now with gas or electricity. Much old iron is needed for making bright new steel.

I'm going down to cut up an old steel ship for use in new steel.

I'm going to same good use. and I will next in the

be cut up for the Maybe the ship both turn up form of a beautiful big new bridge!

A DIVER AND AN OLD IRON STOVE MAY HAVE SOMETHING IN COMMON.

VI

HOW CAN YOU HELP TO SAVE AMERICA?

THE PROPER, saving use of our country's plenty is called conservation. The more everyone knows about conservation, the better for America. You can learn a lot about it from motion picture films. Your school teacher can send for these. Your classes can take trips to watch work being done well and savingly at one place, or wastefully in another. You can write themes about it.

But almost anyone old enough to go to school can do more than merely learn about it. You can do things yourself, directly, to help conservation, and so help save America. This is true whether you live in a city, a smaller town, or out in the open countryside.

If you live in a city

you can save up things for the junkman. He will buy all the old iron you have, including tin cans hammered flat, and sell it to the steel makers. He will buy any other old metals you can find plus old rubber, old rags, cardboard cartons flattened out, as well as newspapers and magazines tied in separate bundles. Old metals will be melted down and made into useful things anew. Old rubber will go into cheaper rubber articles, for which the best grade is not needed.

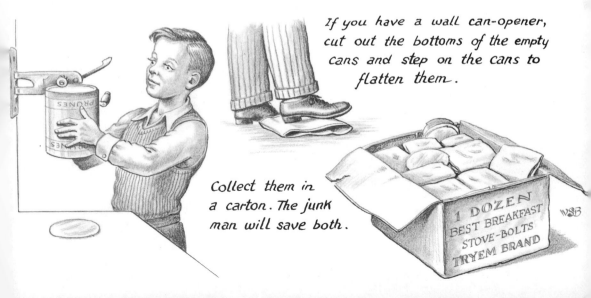

If you have a wall can-opener, cut out the bottoms of the empty cans and step on the cans to flatten them.

Collect them in a carton. The junk man will save both.

Cartons, papers, and rags will become new paper and cartons again. One person alone may not be able to collect a lot of these things. But with all Americans always saving whatever they can, it will add up to a very big saving indeed.

In a city you can help a lot by remembering to turn things off. The gas or electric stove left going, not only wastes the gas or electricity. It may start a terrible fire, with wasteful loss of property, and possibly of life. Much water must be wasted putting it out. Just burning lights when not needed is wasteful. It isn't just your own few lights. It's the millions of lights left burning

all over the country that adds up to a really big waste. Yet, to overcome it, each one must turn off his own few lights. In the city you open handy faucets and water comes out. Do you ever think of the miles and miles of pipes that lead clear back to the reservoir in the distant mountains? You would, if you ever had to pump and carry water from a well, to say nothing of digging the well in the first place.

THIS SORT OF THING IS FUN, AND COMFORTING. BUT YOUR CITY CAN'T AFFORD IT UNLESS THERE HAS BEEN PLENTY OF RAIN AND THE RESERVOIRS ARE FULL.

In the midst of a hot and rainless summer, do you ever say to yourself, "Now is when everybody gets thirsty oftenest, and wants the most baths, and the most clean-washed clothes, and air-conditioning and so forth. But right now the water supply in the city reservoir is at its lowest too. I mustn't run water too fast or too long, or forget to shut it off. And we ought to get a man to fix that leaky faucet. It drips at least a bucket every hour." It isn't just your leaky faucet. It's the thousands of others, also leaking steadly, that adds so to

This way I don't need no ice. I just run cold water on d'milk all day.

the waste. Sometimes, if too many people keep on being careless with water, their city government has to put meters in all buildings, houses, and apartments. Then people pay more and directly for all the water passing through their pipes. It is wonderful how careful they become then—as they should have been all the while.

79

And what about the water where you'd like to swim, the river or the seashore? Can you use it? If not, is it because the city sewers empty there? Is the city garbage dumped there too? If so, you might get up a petition. You might write a letter to the mayor. You could say that your city needs a sewage and garbage treating plant—so that all the children, and everybody else, would have a decent place to swim. Then

80

you could sign your name and get all the children in your block, and all the children in your school, to sign their names under yours, and mail it to the mayor. Mail a copy of the petition to the city editor for him to print in the newspaper too. You might really start something very good and very saving for your special part of America. The mayor of a city has a hard job. Often with too much to do, he may put off things that need attention. Letters from grownups may only make him growl. But he's likely to be a very good fellow at heart. And letters, or a petition, from you and your friends might work wonders.

With a cleaned up river and seashore, picnic areas with room for all might be developed. They would be outdoor refuges of fun and rest for city people. They would save citizens from getting "all worn out." And saving Americans is another good way of saving America. Also there could be more refuge areas for the water-birds and other creatures that surely would return to live in tidal marshes and on river islands. Soon nature-lovers, scientists, and camera fans could

approach the wild things rather closely, so quickly do they
learn where people will not harm them.

Aid to our friends in fur and feathers saves some of our
America too. We cannot all travel to the great National Parks
and wildlife refuges. But many a wonder of nature can be
enjoyed and encouraged even in a city. A wildlife refuge

may cover thousands of square miles, or a small plot of ground, or be one old tree, or the roof of your apartment house, or just one of your apartment windowsills. A city dweller can offer birds resting places, nesting places, nesting materials, food and drink, and a place to bathe. Any one of these comforts may attract birds. And with all together you surely will help some of them. The Superintendent of Documents, Washington 25, D.C., will send you a list of pamphlets on such things as making proper bird houses,

Common Pigeon

House Sparrow

Starling

and attracting birds. Your public library should have books about it also. In winter, in the city, you may get only pigeons, starlings, and sparrow visitors. But even a common pigeon is a splendid bird, his arching neck all a-shimmer with changing colors, his body and wings so streamlined, his feet such a jolly red. The closer you get to a starling the better he looks. He is clad in midnight, and spangled with stars you scarcely see from a distance. City sparrows look best in closeups too, especially the males, with their gray and chestnut caps and black bibs.

CARDINAL

CHICKADEE

BLUE JAY

But you might be surprised to find a jay or cardinal or many another kind of bird at your window refuge, even in the wintertime. Almost any bird you help in winter will pay us all back in the summer. Starlings cruise the countryside for thirty miles around the city, capturing billions of insects as food. Even sparrows, and other birds that eat seeds mostly, feed millions of insects to their growing babies in the nest. Birds get rid of bugs that otherwise would bite us, or spoil our growing food, or kill our forests. The more birds, the fewer bad bugs, and so the more food and lumber saved for our America.

Though living in the city, you can help birds all over the country—by telephone! You can call the program director of

DOWNY WOODPECKER

CHIMNEY SWIFT

HERMIT THRUSH

your local radio station and ask him to urge people everywhere to feed birds during snowy weather. The National Audubon Society, 1006 Fifth Avenue, New York 28, New York, will help you start a Junior Audubon Club at school. Any child can be a member for just ten cents a year. And each member gets six leaflets a year, all about birds. They will help you study birds in city parks, about your home or wherever you may be. You, or your class at school, could join the American Nature Association, 1214 Sixteenth Street, N.W., Washington 6, D.C., and receive their fine monthly magazine.

Maybe your school could have a conservation poster contest. The winning posters, placed in store windows and published in the papers, might really save some of America. A poster telling people to use the ash tray, instead of throwing lighted cigarette butts from their car windows, might do a lot of good. Living where everything is concrete, brick, or stone, city people get careless tobacco habits. When driving in the country, they start many wasteful grass, brush, and forest fires they never even know about. By the time things are really blazing, the careless smoker-tourist is many miles away.

As a Cub or a Brownie, you can join the Boy Scouts or Girl Scouts, or similar groups. Then, perhaps, with a leader, you can go on trips and learn how to enjoy the countryside without spoiling it in any way. Or—

If you live in the suburbs or a smaller town
you can do all the above things and more. You can raise
your own food in a garden. Perhaps you will learn to can
or freeze some of it for winter use. You can have a big boxed-
in compost heap, where you throw a little earth or sand now
and then with all your garden leavings such as corn husks
and carrot tops. They will rot down and make especially
rich soil to put back in the garden. Throw in all the weeds
you pull. Make them put back what they took from your
ground. Dump the garbage there, except the orange, lemon,

and grapefruit skins. These must be burned first, with the rubbish in your incinerator. Otherwise they are too acid and rot too slowly.

When you don't have wood or paper ashes from an incinerator or a fireplace, or coal ashes from a stove or furnace, scatter a little lime on the compost heap once in a while to sweeten it. This will prevent any smell the neighbors would not like, and keep flies away. If food happens to spoil in your pantry, just toss it onto the compost heap. In another year it will be back on the dining table as new vegetables, grown

EMPTY ALL WASTE-BASKETS, CLEAN UP TWIGS FROM LAWN, PLACE CITRUS PEELS ON TOP, AND LIGHT AT BOTTOM.

Cinder-blocks, set up without cement, make a good incinerator in a jiffy.

in richer soil. Rake autumn leaves and add them to the pile. Or if you burn them, put in the ashes. Put in sawdust and the dust from your vacuum cleaner. If you have to trap mice in your cellar, turn them into compost too. Dead plants, dead animals, in fact anything that will decay or burn, can be turned into some fine homemade fertilizer.

By saving some things for the junkman, and by having an incinerator and a compost heap for the garden, you will never be bothered about what to do with garbage and rubbish. You will be making all of it count in your Save America plan. But when you cut the grass, let it lie. It soon

As summer passes, the cuttings, lying layer on layer, form a loose mat - a mulch - that keeps the ground moist longer. By now, last year's cuttings have rotted and are feeding the roots.

ROOTS IN EARTH

will disappear beneath the growing blades and help the lawn. Don't put the cuttings into the compost. That would be robbing the lawn of a lot, to help the garden only a little.

Perhaps your school can have a garden. Maybe your school can have a forest, or your town can. Sometimes, in advertisements, you are urged to ask your parents to buy some special cereal. You are told there is a prize in every package. Why not ask them to stir up the school board or the town board about a forest? There is a much bigger, more

I help re-forest by burying nuts and tree seeds.

So do I!

SHADE FROM THE OLD TREE HELPS SEEDLING TREES WHILE IT HINDERS BRAMBLES.

I may rob your corn-field, but you might sell my fur coat!

WSB

important prize in that. You will be helping save America in a really big way then. A state forester will help you and your parents to improve old woodlands. Here and there he may surprise you by letting stand some of the big old half-dead trees. Full of holes, they are no longer good for lumber. But they provide homes for many a furry beast and for birds—which are good for forests and farms.

The forester will show you how to plant a brand new forest and help you get the little trees. In a few years, as their branches spread, you may need to thin them. This will give more room for those you leave, to grow their very best. If you have planted evergreens, the ones you take out can be sold as Christmas trees. Then will come a stretch of years while you and the young forest are growing up together. Most boys and girls will be the fathers and mothers of other

94

boys and girls some day. By that time the half-grown trees will need thinning again. Some may be cut and sold as posts, poles, or pulp for paper mills. Then when you are grandparents, many fine big trees will be ready for the lumber mill. Only trees that are really ready will be taken. Thus you and your children and their children can enjoy the woods you planted when you were young yourself. And thereafter there will always be plenty of lumber to keep the buildings of your town in good repair, and wood to sell besides.

We cropped the Christmas trees when _I_ was in high school. Your Dad cropped the poles and pulp when _he_ was in high school. Now _you_ are in high school and cropping full-grown trees as they ripen. Your children can do the same.

If you can't arrange for a forest, perhaps you will be allowed to plant new trees along some of your streets and the roads leading into town. Every tree is a gain in wood supply, an aid to wildlife—especially birds—and makes a place more beautiful. See if there isn't a good spot about your home or school for a new tree or some berry-bearing shrubs and hedges. Your State Conservation Department will tell you which kinds provide most food and shelter for birds. And you can send to tree nursery companies for their free illustrated catalogs.

Most birds of prey catch many mice and rats. For this we call them "good". Some kinds, catching other birds, (especially game and poultry), are called "bad". But often it is so hard to tell one kind of hawk from another, that none should be shot unless caught in the act of "chicken stealing". Here are some of our birds of prey as seen overhead, arranged somewhat in the order of their "bad to betterness."

WSB

SPARROW HAWK

GREAT HORNED OWL

GOSHAWK

COOPER'S HAWK

SCREECH OWL

SHARP-SHINNED HAWK

DUCK HAWK

PIGEON HAWK

MARSH HAWK

FROM "BAD"

BARRED OWL

OSPREY

TURKEY VULTURE

SWALLOW-TAILED KITE

BALD EAGLE

BROAD-WINGED HAWK

To BETTER

The more birds we have, the better for America. That is why we have laws to protect them, including most kinds of hawks and owls. They eat insects and mice that otherwise would eat our grass and grain and vegetables. So don't shoot at birds with an air rifle or anything else. It may be more exciting than plinking at tin cans. But it is against the law and the rights of people who want living birds about them, not dead ones. And besides, every bird has as much right to its little share of life as you have to your big share.

97

Don't go close to birds' nests, but from a distance watch them build, brood their eggs, and rear their young. Read some of the many fine books about them. Learn to know the different kinds you see. Keep a list and make notes on the things you see them do, and what you think about it. But never do anything to hinder them. Only do what you can to help them, for they help us all. If you see a baby bird that cannot fly yet, sitting in the road where a car might kill it, or if you fear a cat might catch it, don't "rescue" it and try to raise it. It probably is not lost or orphaned. Put it on a tree branch and go a good way off, or hide and watch. In half an hour at most, you probably will see its mother or father feeding it. Then you will know that all is well.

People should never leave their pets behind when they move away. Dogs and cats have feelings just as we do. They become fond of us, and learn to count on us for food and friendship and a home. Then suddenly—if we are pet deserters—they find we can't be counted on. They can only rely on themselves. A few, by sheer good luck, may find better homes with kinder people. But often, after much unhappy straying, they either starve or turn wild. Such a dog will catch and eat whatever he can, from ground-nesting birds to deer, if he is big enough. Such a cat will catch more mice in the woods and fields, but more birds also. Kind people and good conservationists do not desert pet animals.

Desertion turned these dogs into a "wolf-pack." They destroy wildlife.

Are there any dirt roads in your town? Are there many unpaved roads in the country round-about? We are losing soil from those roads every time it rains. It is washed down the ditches, into the streams, and away. Are there stretches of road that wash out and must be filled in over and over with dirt? Are there places where holes develop? You could gather enough small stones to fill a few holes level. That might prevent some wasteful accidents.

Then you might go to the next town meeting with a grown-up relative or friend. You might stand up and tell what little you were able to do by yourself. But you could

say that such roads are not well-graded, that more dirt roads should be paved. And all ditches should be planted with grass to keep soil from washing away. You could ask what the town will do about it. You could say you and the other children will have to live in the town a lot longer than the grownups. So how about fixing things up? Sometimes it takes something like that to jog people into doing their part to help save America. But at least, in our free nation, no one needs to be afraid to say just what he thinks.

Many grownups may laugh to hear a boy or girl speak up at meeting. They won't be laughing at you. They will be

feeling foolish for not thinking of what you said themselves.
If you live in a small town or on a farm,
you may have the most chances of all to help save America.
You can do most of the things mentioned so far, plus many
more. By the time you are nine, you can join a 4-H club and
learn a lot about conservation first hand, right out in the
country. You can learn how to raise the finest farm animals
and vegetables. This is not only good for our nation, but
you may make money and win prizes as well. And you have
the fine feeling of success in good work well done. Almost

anywhere in the country you still can look around you and see land being wasted. Farmer X, up the road from your home—is he still plowing up and down his sloping fields? Does he still plant corn and other things in rows running up and down? Does he leave hilly fields bare all winter? Does he spread the precious barnyard manure there, only to have most of it carried away down the rows when the spring rains come? Are gullies cutting ever deeper into his fields as more and more soil washes away? Next time you go to a big conservation show, where they fix up a mistreated, run-down farm in one day, invite Farmer X to go with you and your family. He needs to see it more than you do.

Farther up the road is there a deserted farm where the land is so worn out that crops won't grow at all any more? Trees would. If the place was planted with baby trees a forest would grow. Slowly but steadily it would improve the soil. And meantime, it would make more living room for wild creatures. The more space for wildlife, the more wildlife for us to enjoy in our various ways—nature students all the year, hunters in the lawful seasons.

Planting trees and hedges is good business in the country. In summer, low trees and shrubs around the fields are per-

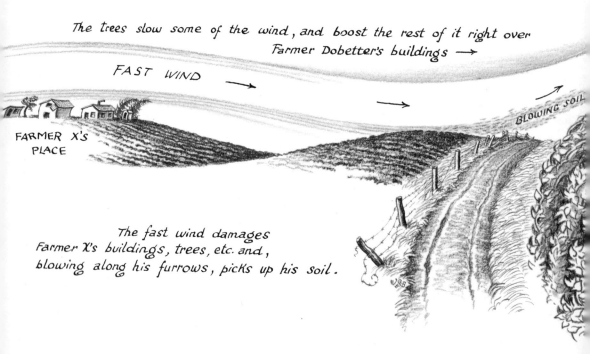

The trees slow some of the wind, and boost the rest of it right over Farmer Dobetter's buildings →

FAST WIND →

FARMER X'S PLACE

BLOWING SOIL

The fast wind damages Farmer X's buildings, trees, etc. and, blowing along his furrows, picks up his soil.

manent guide-lines for the wise farmer, who plows level furrows on his slopes. They keep the wind from blowing farm soil away. They help keep soil where it belongs in wet weather too. In winter, such windbreaks catch and bank the snow, holding more moisture for the land. Along the road they act as permanent snow-fences. One kind of rose hedge, called "living fence," keeps livestock in their proper fields better than posts and barbed wire, and with no upkeep. Small birds nest in it, protected by its many thorns. In winter they feed on its little rose apples.

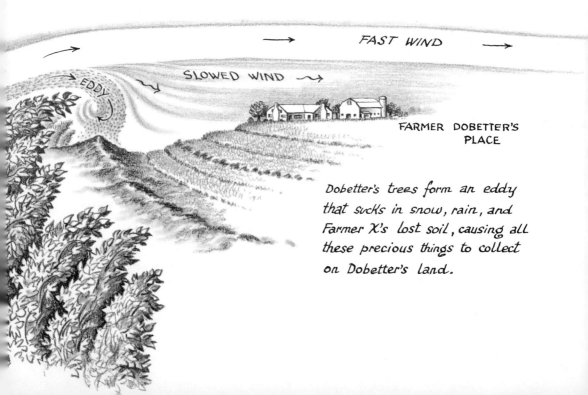

FAST WIND

SLOWED WIND

EDDY

FARMER DOBETTER'S PLACE

Dobetter's trees form an eddy that sucks in snow, rain, and Farmer X's lost soil, causing all these precious things to collect on Dobetter's land.

Are there trees along that meadow stream? They would
keep it from cutting its banks. Without trees it snakes all over
the land, making its pebbly bed ever wider, carrying away
pasture soil. Trees would keep the water cooler too, and
better for fishes. They would give comforting shade for

people who just like to sit and fish. For livelier people they would be fun to jump from into the old swimming hole.

Willows are easiest to plant, and they grow very quickly. Just take shoots from a willow tree already grown, and stick them into the muddy banks about six feet apart. The leaves will wither but roots will sprout. Soon new leaves will grow and the little trees will be well started. Or you can keep your shoots in water in the shade till they sprout roots, before you plant them. This sounds very easy. But, as with so many things, it may not be so simple. Cows, except for special drinking places, must be fenced off from the stream. They eat tender willows. If muskrats live in the stream, they may pull up your shoots. A wire sleeve around each shoot might solve this problem. So might mothballs. People are, perhaps, the only animals that don't mind them. Try pressing two or three into the mud, about six inches from each shoot, as an experiment.

Just what I like for breakfast!

IN THE SHADE

Weeping willows
grow even faster
than common ones—
and never die of
blight.

Grass-grown spillway ——→

Is your uncle planning to drain the big swamp on his farm, to get more space for growing corn? It would be a pity to do all that work, only to find that the soil there isn't fit to grow such crops. A government expert, testing it first, might save a lot of trouble. Maybe, instead of draining the swamp, cypress trees, or rice, or cranberries could be grown there, according to your climate. Maybe some of it could be deepened for a fish pond.

Probably, if the swamp were drained, that steady little spring in the pasture below would stop flowing. At present the cows have a mucky time all trying to drink from it at

Some of the swamp turned into a cranberry bog—

←grass-grown spillway

once. Why not make the pond right there about the spring? From the lower side of such a pond, water could be piped to an ample drinking trough. In the pond you could raise fishes, furnished by your State Fish Hatchery. You could swim there in summer, and skate in winter. In one summer day, a bulldozer might fix the pond. By the following spring it would be ready for all of its good uses.

Some farmers keep their orchard land bare, turning the soil over again and again with a disc-harrow. They say that loose soil at the surface keeps moisture in the ground beneath. A good turf would do this better, and no soil would blow or wash away with the rain. And turf makes a softer, cleaner place for fruit to fall. What's more, orchard grass can be mowed for hay.

However, in winter, in grassy orchards, hungry field mice and rabbits are liable to gnaw the bark of fruit trees. If twigs and branches from the fall trimming are left on the ground, the mice and rabbits will work on these for a while. But later they may try their teeth on the trunks. This can kill the trees. It's a bother and expense to band every trunk with small meshed wire netting. Again as an experiment, why not try laying a ring of mothballs, two inches apart, around each tree? The mice detest them. So may the rabbits, and they last for months.

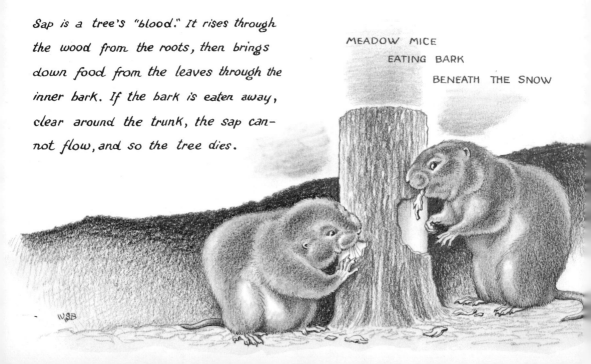

Sap is a tree's "blood." It rises through the wood from the roots, then brings down food from the leaves through the inner bark. If the bark is eaten away, clear around the trunk, the sap cannot flow, and so the tree dies.

MEADOW MICE
EATING BARK
BENEATH THE SNOW

Meadowlark

Out in the hay fields, do you know where meadow larks are nesting? You could help both them and the farmer a lot by marking the nests with sticks when the hay is to be cut. You could, that is, if the farmer would leave a little "island" of uncut grass around each nest, and not run through it with the mower. For sparing their lives, the nestlings and the parent birds would repay him many times. They would eat thousands and thousands of grasshoppers, beetles, and beetle grubs that would otherwise eat his grass.

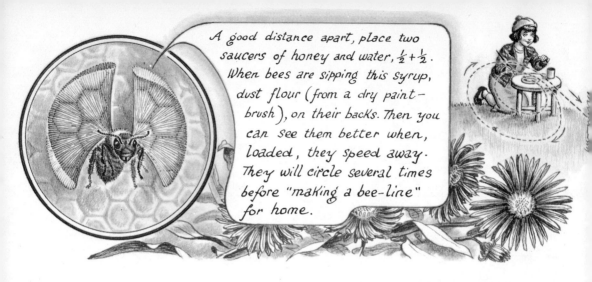

A good distance apart, place two saucers of honey and water, $\frac{1}{2} + \frac{1}{2}$. When bees are sipping this syrup, dust flour (from a dry paint-brush), on their backs. Then you can see them better when, loaded, they speed away. They will circle several times before "making a bee-line" for home.

Seldom if ever would the birds eat any bees. And this is good, because bees also help with the farming. They help flowering trees and plants produce their fruit and vegetables. They help the clover and alfalfa fields produce their seed. And they themselves produce delicious honey. Sometimes, instead of using the farmer's hives, bees go wild and make their honey in a hollow tree out in the woods. Generally such a tree is cut down and the hive destroyed to get the honey. But if it were not felled, the same bee-tree might furnish honey time and time again. Some one handy with carpenter's

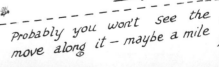

Probably you won't see the move along it — maybe a mile

Where two bee-lines meet, you will find the bee-tree (or maybe a bee-keeper's hives.)

Before your man with the tools begins, he can learn from a bee-keeper, or a book at your library, how to get honey out of a hive, wild or tame, without getting stung.

tools could neatly open one side of the trunk with a saw and chisel. Then, after taking out some honey and leaving some —bees always make much more than they need for themselves—the chunk of trunk could be replaced with hinges and a padlock, like a door. This way, with their home unharmed, wild bees will go right on making fine food for us, just like tame ones. Some calm autumn morning, see if you can find a bee-tree, in the way shown in the picture.

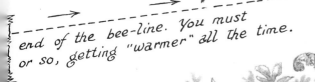

end of the bee-line. You must or so, getting "warmer" all the time.

A BEE-SMOKER

VII

EVERYTHING MAKES A DIFFERENCE

SOMETIMES you may feel that what little you can do for conservation will not count for much. Yet it will. It surely will. For actually no one works alone, and nothing is ever done quite separately from other things. Small deeds may seem like trifles, but taken together, they can make tremendous differences.

We have seen how important a small thing like a bee is to a big thing like an apple tree. Unless it carries pollen dust from blossom to blossom, there will be no fruit. So the bee, as well as the tree, is important to the farmer—and to us. The farmer can sell the apples and buy chicken-feed; we can buy the apples and eat them.

Just as surely as bees and trees are important, so is everything else in this world, however large or small. Everything counts, everything makes a difference to everything else, from the great sun to the tiniest invisible atom. There is power in everything. The sun's power is good for us, or deadly, according to how much we get of its light and heat. The same is true of the atom, according to what use we make of it. Between the mighty sun and the mighty atom, there is

LIFE AT THE SHORE

The Sun's rays with shade, water, and drinks

or

DEATH IN THE DESERT
without shade or water

ATOM BOMB TEST

ANOTHER KIND OF DEATH IN THE DESERT

The Atom's power in deadly bombs, or in better devices for better living,—

← ATOMIC AID IN LEARNING ANSWERS TO LIFE'S DEEPEST SECRETS

50,000 miles
of the Sun's surface

"Spots" on the Sun show where cyclones, great whirling, fiery, electronic storms are raging. In years when there are many sun-spots we have electric changes on our Planet Earth. There is much radio interference and telegraph trouble, while compasses on ships and planes don't point true, – and we have especially fine displays of Northern Lights.

But perhaps most important, we have long droughts. It is believed that, in heavy sun-spot years, people are more active and have shorter tempers !

power in everything else, including ourselves. And whatever you, or anyone, or anything does or does not do, makes a difference. It makes a difference how your power, everybody's and everything's power is used.

If there is a storm on the sun, it makes a difference in the weather here on the earth. And the weather makes a mighty difference to us all. We may have good crops or poor, according to the weather. We may be overcome with heat, or freeze to death, or just be comfortable, according to the weather.

116

People don't have the power in themselves to control the weather. We can't make it rain whenever we please, or stop the raining when we want to. But, working together with our many good minds and able hands, we do have the power to store and save water for dry times, to use water wisely in good times, and to keep flooding water from doing much harm in wet times. The difference depends on what we do or do not do about it.

Anyone can see that water is important. It is easy to see that we must have a plan for its proper use. But what about things that are not planned? What about accidents? What about, say, that skunk lying dead beside the highway, killed by a motor car? In starting to cross the road, it tried to do something but did not succeed. Except to the unlucky skunk, does that make a difference? Is that important to anything or anybody else? Well, yes. The skunk's failure matters to

CONTROLLING
WEATHER IS
VERY "IFFY"

I could make it rain if there were any clouds today, if I had the right chemicals to spray them, if I had a plane, if I could fly it.

the farmer in whose woods it lived, though he will probably not realize it. The farmer may only think that if there had been no accident he might have trapped the skunk and sold the fur. More likely he will think that, dead, the skunk can no longer squirt a horrible smelling liquid on him, if he doesn't watch out, and that it is no longer a possible danger to his poultry.

But the living skunk was important too, in ways the farmer never realized, possibly. First, it spent much time digging beetle-grubs out of the farmer's soil. Beetle-grubs can ruin a hay field or pasture by eating the roots of the grasses. Second, the skunk often ate grown-up beetles also. These never got a chance to lay more eggs to hatch more grubs. Third, in the fall, thousands of grasshoppers laid about thirty eggs apiece in the farmer's fields. But the skunk spent many a night digging them up and eating them. Thus, the next summer there was no pest of new grasshoppers eating the grass and clover. Fourth, except in the worst winter months, the skunk caught field mice for a part of its fare. This also saved the farmer's grass from being eaten by the mice.

We may be only beetles, but "among other things" we eat _skunks_ — dead ones, that is. Also we will bury a dead mouse or bird by digging the earth from under it till it sinks from sight. Then we dig down and lay eggs on the body. When our grubs hatch, they feed on it. "Nothing goes for nothing"— is right!

VERY DEAD

SHREW

BURYING BEETLES

W&B

Even now, though dead, the skunk is still important. When the highway traffic lets up long enough, a hungry buzzard may carry the body to a nearby field, to dine in greater safety. Carrion-beetles will feast on what the big bird leaves. The little bones will sink from sight among the clover. They will enrich and sweeten the soil. The clover there will be better because of them. Bees will get more nectar from the blossoms. And later on, the farmer's cow, standing in the barn in wintertime, will enjoy an especially sweet forkful of clover-hay. Who knows, being so pleased, she may let down an extra pint of milk that day. About here we lose track of the skunk's small body. But we see that it has never left off being of importance to the living world. For everything does make some difference to everything else.

And everything is always changing, rapidly enough to see in a molting insect, for example; or too slowly to notice, as in a granite boulder. It may take hundreds or thousands of years for sun and frost to crack the rock. But always the changing weather weakens it. One day it will have crumbled and become a part of the soil in which things grow.

Shortly after a Cicada climbs out of its first wingless armor, two little pads, unfolding on its shoulders, grow into wings before your very eyes, a rapid change.

OLD
ARMOR

1

2

But you may have great-grandchildren before you see this tree crack the rock clear through.

I WILL CRUMBLE

I WILL GROW

I WILL BE PAPER

I WILL BE A BOOK

I WILL BE READ (I HOPE)

FREEDOM AND PLENTY OURS to SAVE

1   2   3   4   5

Suppose that not so long ago, a tree was growing in soil that once was rock. Suppose the tree was cut for use in making paper. Suppose that the paper was used to make this very book. The more this book is read, the more people may change, from being wasteful to using things more carefully and wisely. But also, the more this book is used, the more it too will change, becoming ever more tattered and torn. There may come a day when, utterly used up and worn out, it lies at last in a compost heap. The compost, used in a garden, will make bigger and better tomatoes. Somebody else reading some other book and eating one of those fine tomatoes, will not know that this book helped to make it taste so good. But it will be so just the same.

So it goes. You can think of many more examples of things that are important to a long list of other things. We can't control the weather or keep it, or anything else, from changing a lot or a little all the time. But we can work with nature instead of against it, and make good saving use of all things, even as they change. And in doing so, every American is important. For each one of us has a part of the power needed to help save America. Indeed, all working together, we have the power not only to save America, but to help save the world.

Shall we save America? Who would answer no? For who would give up freedom and plenty, which together make our happiness? Shall we help save the world? Shall we help the friendly people of other nations whose lands are poorer than our own, wherever and whenever we can? The answer still is yes. For only when there is freedom and plenty for everyone the world over, will the happiness of anyone, anywhere, be truly safe.

THE END

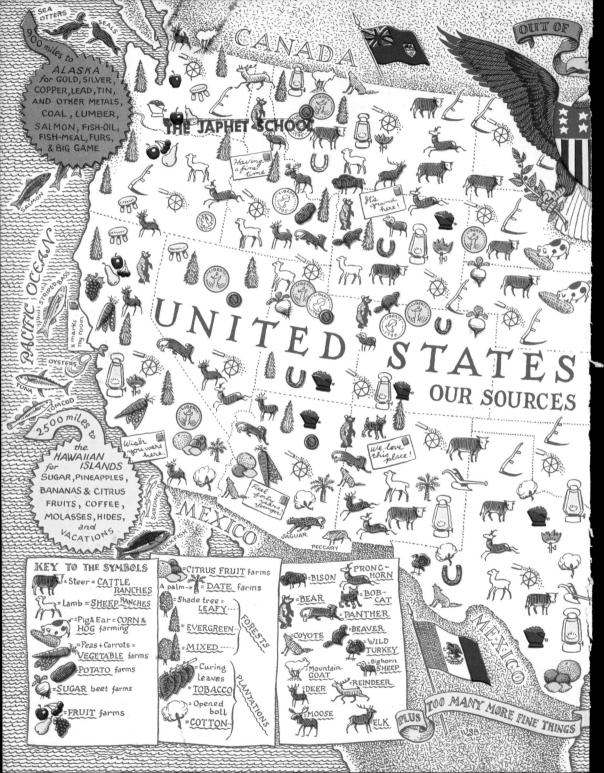